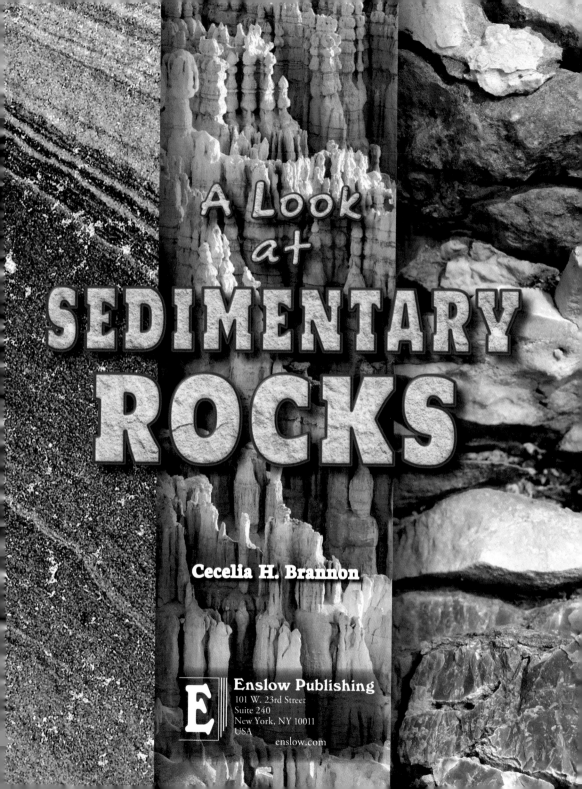

A Look at
SEDIMENTARY
ROCKS

Cecelia H. Brannon

Enslow Publishing
101 W. 23rd Street
Suite 240
New York, NY 10011
USA

enslow.com

Published in 2016 by Enslow Publishing, LLC
101 W. 23rd Street, Suite 240, New York, NY 10011

Library of Congress Cataloging-in-Publication Data
Brannon, Cecelia H., author.
 A look at sedimentary rocks / Cecelia H. Brannon.
    pages cm. — (The rock cycle)
 Audience: Ages 8+
 Audience: Grades 4 to 6.
 Includes bibliographical references and index.
 ISBN 978-0-7660-7338-8 (library binding)
 ISBN 978-0-7660-7336-4 (pbk.)
 ISBN 978-0-7660-7337-1 (6-pack)
 1. Sedimentary rocks—Juvenile literature. 2. Geochemical cycles—Juvenile literature. I. Title.
 QE471.B76 2016
 552.5—dc23
                              2015029182

Printed in the United States of America

To Our Readers: We have done our best to make sure all websites in this book were active and appropriate when we went to press. However, the author and the publisher have no control over and assume no liability for the material available on those websites or any websites they may link to. Any comments or suggestions can be sent by e-mail to customerservice@enslow.com.

Photo Credits: Throughout book: steve estvanik/Shutterstock.com (red Navajo sandstone), Weldon Schloneger/Shutterstock.com (blue chert), bikeriderlondon/Shutterstock.com (Paria Canyon-Vermilion Cliffs sandstone), Christine Yarusi (series logo, four-rock dingbat), optimarc/Shutterstock.com (chalcedony stone background); cover, p. 1 Robert Adrian Hillman/Shutterstock.com (left), dibrova/Shutterstock.com (center), dexns/Shutterstock.com (right), Kues/Shutterstock.com (book title texture); p. 4 www.sandatlas.org/Shutterstock.com; p.7 Aaron Rutten/Shutterstock.com; p. 8 ZeWrestler/Wikimedia Commons/Rockcycle2.jpg/public domain; p. 10 Paco Toscano/Shutterstock.com; p. 11 CHAIWATPHOTOS/Shutterstock.com; p. 12 Nina B/Shutterstock.com; p. 13 elnavegante/Shutterstock.com; p. 14 amornchaij/Shutterstock.com; p. 16 Photo Image/Shutterstock.com; p. 17 Elena Elisseeva/Shutterstock.com; p. 19 sonsam/Shutterstock.com (top), Tyler Boyes/Shutterstock.com (bottom); p. 20 oksana2010/Shutterstock.com; p. 21 MarcelClemens/Shutterstock.com; p. 22 Platslee/Shutterstock.com; p. 23 K-Mike/Shutterstock.com; p. 24 Zack Frank/Shutterstock.com (top), Yuri Megel/Shutterstock.com (bottom); p. 26 Pichugin Dmitry/Shutterstock.com; p. 27 Adam J/Shutterstock.com (top), George W.Bailey/Shutterstock.com (bottom); p. 29, suronin/Shutterstock.com.

Contents

These cliffs in Red Canyon State Park in California are made from colorful layers of sedimentary rock.

What SEDIMENTARY ROCKS ARE

Rocks come in a variety of colors, shapes, sizes, and materials. They are constantly changing and help shape the Earth's surface. All rocks on Earth can be classified into three groups: **igneous rocks**, **metamorphic rocks**, and **sedimentary rocks**.

Pressed Layers

Sedimentary rocks are formed when mud, sand, or smaller bits of rock are pressed together. As these bits of **sediment** are pressed together, they form layers, called **strata**. Over time, the weight of the upper layers creates pressure on the lower layers, which compacts them together. These compressed strata create sedimentary rocks.

The Rock Cycle

The creation of sedimentary rocks is part of the rock cycle. The rock cycle is the process by which rocks are formed and then broken down by wind, water, or ice. Over time, pressure, heat, and other forces help the pieces of rock and other matter form new rocks.

The creation of new rocks by the rock cycle occurs in Earth's layers. Beneath Earth's crust is the mantle, a layer of hot liquid rock called magma. This magma is pushed to Earth's surface, where it cools and hardens to create igneous rocks. These rocks are worn down over time by forces such as wind and water. The wind and water break off tiny particles, called sediment, of the igneous rocks. This sediment is deposited then pressed together to form sedimentary rocks. When pressure and heat change the minerals in igneous and sedimentary rocks, they form metamorphic rocks. Earthquakes and other movements push the igneous, sedimentary, and metamorphic rocks below Erath's crust, where magma melts them. They rise to the surface to make new rocks again.

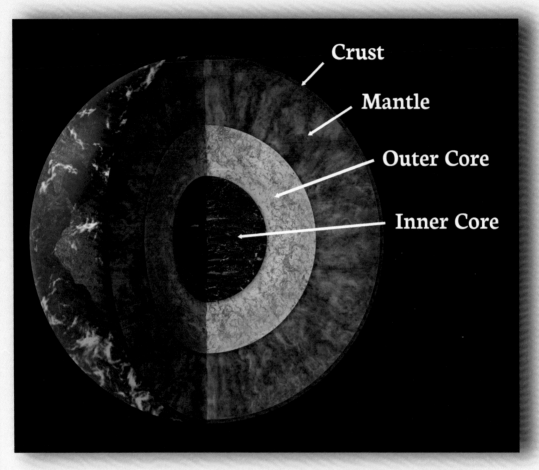

Crust

Mantle

Outer Core

Inner Core

Earth is made of layers. The top layer (where we live) is called the crust. It is made from rock and soil. Under the crust is a thick layer of magma called the mantle. Below the mantle is Earth's core, which has two layers. The outer core is made from melted metal, while the inner core is a solid metal ball.

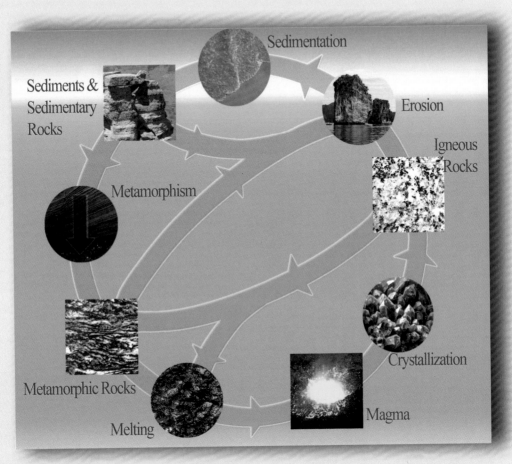

Sedimentation

Sediments & Sedimentary Rocks

Erosion

Igneous Rocks

Metamorphism

Metamorphic Rocks

Crystallization

Melting

Magma

This diagram shows how the rock cycle works to create new rocks from old rocks. When a lot of pressure is applied to sediment, it forms sedimentary rocks.

The Formation of
SEDIMENTARY
ROCKS

There are five processes involved in the creation of sedimentary rocks: weathering, erosion, transportation, deposition, and lithification. These are all part of the rock cycle and part of how the Earth's surface is shaped.

Weathering

Weathering is the process that wears down rock. There are two types of weathering.

Physical, or mechanical, weathering occurs when physical forces wear down a rock. For example, wind can blow bits of matter against a sedimentary rock, which breaks it down over time.

The east coast of
Gran Canaria in the
Canary Islands, Spain,
shows all the steps
in the formation of
sedimentary rocks.

Did You Know?

Eight percent of Earth's crust is made of sedimentary rocks, the majority of which are mountains, cliffs, and volcanoes.

Chemical weathering occurs when forces, such as water, change a rock's minerals into different minerals. Elements are added or removed from the minerals, which weakens the rock. This occurs when minerals in sedimentary rocks absorb water. The water breaks down the rock from the inside.

This trail in Moab, Utah, was created through the process of weathering. Here, you can see the snow and ice eroding sediment from the rocks.

Did You Know?

This geological formation is called The Submarine. It is in Ischigualasto Natural Park in San Juan, Argentina. Its unique shape was created through the weathering process in the rock cycle.

This waterfall in Thailand shows one way
in which rocks can be eroded.

The FORMATION of SEDIMENTARY ROCKS

Erosion

Erosion is the process of rock wearing away, traveling, and being left behind to form sediment. After rocks are worn down through weathering, they are often fragmented into smaller pieces. These pieces travel through water and wind. Bits of rock, grains of sand, and other matter mix together to form sediment.

Once the sediment has formed, it travels through various streams and rivers. The waves in the water move the sediment around. Sediment is heavier than water, so it sinks. Lighter pieces settle on top of the heavier ones. The largest and heaviest pieces fall to the bottom, while the lightest pieces settle on the top. Sediment is constantly washing into the ocean and adding new layers to its floor.

Erosion, like weathering, can be caused by different natural elements. Rainwater falls against sedimentary rocks and washes away the already weak and weathered pieces. The water in rivers and streams then sweeps up these rock pieces. In time, they end up settling into layers at the bottom of the ocean. Both weathering and erosion have important roles in the formation of sedimentary rocks. They help create and move sediment.

Transportation and Deposition

Transportation is the process by which sediment moves from one place to another. Just like you may ride in a car or on a train to get to school, sediment moves from place to place using transportation. For sediment, transportation means running water (like a stream or river), ice (like a melting glacier), or wind.

The Mississippi River carries many pieces of sediment to new places.

When the water, ice, or wind drops the sediment after transportation, it is called deposition. This could be in a river, on land, or on a glacier depending on how heavy the sediment is.

Lithification

Lithification is the process in which pressure is applied to layers of **debris** over millions of years to form new sedimentary rocks. The process begins when layers of sediment are added to one another through erosion. The added layers put more pressure on the bottom layer of sediment. This pressure pushes out any water that may be in the sediment. Taking out the water makes it easier for the minerals in the sediment to be pushed together. When the minerals are pushed together, they change and harden. It

This canyon in Alberta, Canada, was created by years of sediment collecting under pressure.

takes millions of years for layers of sediment to harden into sedimentary rock. The layers of sediment have to be about one half to two miles (one to three kilometers) deep to create enough pressure to form sedimentary rock.

Types of
SEDIMENTARY
ROCKS

There are three types of sedimentary rocks: clastic, biochemical or organic, and chemical. They are classified by what they are made of and how they are formed.

Clastic Rocks

Clastic rocks are the largest group of sedimentary rocks. They are made up of pieces of rock and matter, such as mud, called clasts. Conglomerates are clastic rocks made of smooth pebbles. They are stuck together through the process of lithification with other kinds of sediment, such as sand or clay. Water moves over the pebbles to wear away the edges, which makes them smooth and round.

Types of **SEDIMENTARY ROCKS**

This conglomerate rock is made from pebbles stuck together and smoothed out by water.

Breccia, another clastic rock, is also formed from rocks stuck together. Unlike those in conglomerates, the rocks in breccia are sharp and rough. The rocks that form breccia did not travel in water long enough to become smooth.

This is an example of a breccia sedimentary rock. It is made of smaller rocks bound together through pressure.

Organic Sedimentary Rocks

An organic rock is formed from fossils, or the remains of dead creatures. The bottom of a lake or an ocean is covered with shells of tiny sea animals that lived there millions of years ago. Over time, these shells can be pushed down by the layers of sediment above them.

Some of these shells contain calcite, which forms a sedimentary rock called limestone. Limestone is usually white, gray, or black. Sometimes you can see tiny pieces of shells inside a piece of limestone rock. These shell pieces are so small that they can only be seen under a microscope.

Did You Know?

Chalk is made of limestone.

Chemical Sedimentary Rocks

Most sedimentary rocks are formed from layers of sediment under pressure. However, some sedimentary rocks form when minerals break down in water. This type of sedimentary rock is chemically formed.

Did You Know?

Many organically formed sedimentary rocks contain fossils. Most plants and animals rot away or are eaten by other animals. However, if a plant or animal is buried quickly by sediment, it can become a fossil, such as the fish pictured below. Fossils in a rock can tell scientists which creatures lived on Earth millions of years ago.

The white cliffs of Dover in the UK are famous for their white chalky appearance. It is limestone that makes them look this way.

Did you Know?

If you've ever used salt to season your food, you've used the chemical sedimentary rock halite! Halite is formed deep underground, and particles of it are released into water when it dissolves. This is what makes ocean water salty!

Caves

Have you ever been inside a cave? Rocks hang from the ceiling and shoot up from the floor. These rock formations, called **stalactites** and **stalagmites** are chemically formed sedimentary rocks. Caves are often made of limestone, the most common of sedimentary rocks.

Limestone contains a mineral called calcite. When water seeps through limestone, it breaks down the calcite. In time, the water disappears and leaves behind a calcite deposit. The calcite deposit hardens into rocks. Stalagmites form from the calcite deposit that builds up from the drips onto the floor of a cave. Stalactites form when the calcite hangs from the ceiling.

Mammoth Cave in Kentucky is one of the longest caves in the world and covers more than 340 miles (547 km). Despite its size, the cave actually got its name from the remains of a woolly mammoth that archeologists found inside.

Agate

Sometimes water collects in small holes in the ground. If a mineral called quartz is in these holes, a sedimentary rock called agate can form. The water breaks down the quartz and creates agate. Agate forms in layers and is very smooth. Agate often forms inside geodes, which are hollow round sedimentary rocks.

Geodes look like normal rocks on the outside, but inside are layers of color!

How SEDIMENTARY ROCKS Are Used

Many sedimentary rocks are useful. Limestone has been used for building for thousands of years. It can be heated and ground into cement. Soil that contains high levels of limestone is used for growing crops. Because much of limestone is made from organic materials, it makes the soil rich in nutrients.

Coal is a sedimentary rock that is made of plants. When plants waste away, they become sediment. Pressure changes the sediment into coal. At one time, buildings all over the world were heated by coal.

Did You Know?

The Pyramids of Giza in Egypt are made from limestone. They were built more than five thousand years ago and are still standing today.

You may have seen trucks spreading rock salt to melt ice and snow in the winter. Rock salt is made from sedimentary rocks.

People in ancient times used a sedimentary rock called flint to make tools. They also rubbed together pieces of flint to start a fire.

Coal is a
sedimentary
rock that
is used for
fuel.

These ancient arrowheads are made of flint.

Why SEDIMENTARY ROCKS Are Important

Besides being useful in everyday life, sedimentary rocks are also important to science. Scientists can study sedimentary rocks to see the layers of sediment that formed them. Studying the rock layers helps scientists discover how Earth formed and how much it has changed over the years. Sedimentary rocks also hold clues to how old Earth really is. Fossils trapped in these rocks tell scientists which creatures lived on Earth millions of years ago. Scientists can also study sedimentary rocks from different parts of the world to see what Earth looked like long ago.

The Danxia landform in China was created by the compression of red sandstone and other minerals. It dates back to the Cretaceous age (145.5 million years ago).

Earth would be a very different place without sedimentary rocks. For millions of years, they have given the rock cycle the pieces needed to make new rocks and shape Earth's surface. They will continue to be an important part of the rock cycle for millions more.

Glossary

conglomerates—Types of sedimentary rocks made of rounded rock pieces that are stuck together.

debris—Particles washed off during the erosion process that are carried by water and/or wind.

erosion—The breaking down and moving of rocks and other matter by natural forces.

igneous rocks—Hot liquid underground minerals that have cooled and hardened into rocks.

lithification—The process of changing layers of sediment into sedimentary rock.

metamorphic rocks—Rocks that have been changed by heat and heavy weight.

sediment—Sand or mud carried by wind or water.

sedimentary rocks—Layers of gravel, sand, or mud that have been pressed together to form rocks.

stalactites—Creations made by water and rock that hang down from the ceilings of caves.

stalagmites—Creations made by water and rock that rise up from the ground.

strata—The layers in sedimentary rocks,

weathering—The breaking down of rocks through natural forces.

Further Reading

Coleman, Miriam. *Investigating Sedimentary Rocks*. New York: PowerKids Press, 2015.

Conklin, Wendy. *The Rock Cycle*. Teacher Created Materials, 2015.

Hirsch, Rebecca E. *Sedimentary Rocks*. Mankato, Minn.: ABDO, 2015.

Lindeen, Mary. *Investigating the Rock Cycle*. Minneapolis, Minn.: Lerner Classroom, 2015.

WEBSITES

Science Kids
sciencekids.co.nz/sciencefacts/earth/sedimentaryrocks.html
Learn more about sedimentary rocks.

Geology.com
geology.com/rocks/sedimentary-rocks.shtml
Learn about different types of sedimentary rocks.

One Geology Kids
onegeology.org/extra/kids/sedimentary.html
Learn more about geoscience, the rock cycle, and sedimentary rocks.

Index